P9-DHN-465

Fitchburg Public Library
610 Main Street
Fitchburg, MA 01420

NIGHT OF THE REPUBLIC

Books by Alan Shapiro

Night of the Republic

ALAN SHAPIRO

Houghton Mifflin Harcourt
Boston   New York   2012

Copyright © 2012 by Alan Shapiro

ALL RIGHTS RESERVED

For information about permission to reproduce selections from this book, write to Permissions, Houghton Mifflin Harcourt Publishing Company, 215 Park Avenue South, New York, New York 10003.

www.hmhbooks.com

Library of Congress Cataloging-in-Publication Data
Shapiro, Alan, date.
  Night of the republic : poems / Alan Shapiro.
    p. cm.
  Includes bibliographical references.
  ISBN 978-0-547-32970-3
  I. Title.
  PS3569.H338N54 2012
  811'.54—dc22   2010049850

Book design by Patrick Barry

Printed in the United States of America

DOC 10 9 8 7 6 5 4 3 2 1

The author thanks the following journals, in which these poems, or versions of them, first appeared: *Bellevue Literary Review:* "Galaxy Formation." *Burnside Review:* "Race Track," "Barbershop." *Forward:* "Dry Cleaner," "Senior Center." *New Ohio Review:* "Indoor Municipal Pool," "Downtown Strip Club." *New Republic:* "Car Dealership," "The Public," "Government Center." *The New Yorker:* "Solitaire." *Ploughshares:* "Bookstore," "Park Bench," "Stone Church." *Poetry:* "Gas Station Restroom," "Supermarket," "Bedroom Door," "Sickbed." *Slate:* "Triumph." *Smartish Pace:* "Close to You," "Edenic Simile." *Tikkun:* "Convention Hall."

"Municipal Pool" was selected for *The Pushcart Prize XXXV: Best of the Small Presses* (2011).

I also wish to thank the Institute for the Arts and Humanities at the University of North Carolina for a fellowship that gave me time to write several of these poems. And as always much gratitude and love to the friends whose criticism has made this book so much better than it otherwise would have been.

For Reg Gibbons

Contents

III. NIGHT OF THE REPUBLIC

IV. AT THE CORNER OF
COOLIDGE AND CLARENCE

I

NIGHT OF THE REPUBLIC

Gas Station Restroom

The present tense
is the body's past tense
here; hence
the ghost sludge of hands
on the now gray strip
of towel hanging limp
from the jammed dispenser;
hence the mirror
squinting through grime
at grime, and the worn-
to-a-sliver of soiled soap
on the soiled sink.
The streaked bowl,
the sticky toilet seat, air
claustral with stink —
all residues and traces
of the ancestral
spirit of body free
of spirit — hence,
behind the station,
at the back end of the store,
hidden away
and dimly lit
this cramped and
solitary carnival
inversion — Paul
becoming Saul

becoming scents
anonymous
and animal; hence,
over the insides
of the lockless stall
the cave-like
scribblings and glyphs
declaring unto all
who come to it
in time: "heaven
is here at hand
and dark, and hell
is odorless; hell
is bright and clean."

Car Dealership at 3 A.M.

Over the lot a sodium aura
within which
above the new cars sprays
of denser many-colored brightnesses
are rising and falling in a time lapse
of a luminous and ghostly
garden forever flourishing
up out of its own decay.

The cars, meanwhile, modest as angels
or like angelic
hoplites, are arrayed
in rows, obedient to orders
they bear no trace of,
their bodies taintless, at attention,
serving the sheen they bear,
the glittering they are,
the sourceless dazzle
that the showcase window
that the showroom floor
weeps for
when it isn't there —

like patent leather, even the black wheels shine.

Here is the intense
amnesia of the just now

at last no longer longing
in a flowering of lights
beyond which
one by one, haphazardly
the dented, the rusted-through,
metallic Eves and Adams
hurry past, as if ashamed,
their dull beams averted,
low in the historical dark they disappear into.

Supermarket

The one cashier is dozing —
head nodding, slack mouth open,
above the cover girl spread out before her on the counter
smiling up
with indiscriminate forgiveness
and compassion for everyone
who isn't her.

Only the edge
is visible of the tightly spooled
white miles
of what is soon
to be the torn-off-
inch-by-inch receipts,
and the beam of green light in the black glass
of the self-scanner
drifts free in the space that is the sum
of the cost of all the items that tonight
won't cross its path.

Registers of feeling too precise
too intricate to feel
except in the disintegrating
traces of a dream —
panopticon of cameras
cutting in timed procession
from aisle to aisle

to aisle on the overhead screens
above the carts asleep inside each other —
above the darkened
service desk, the pharmacy, the nursery,
so everywhere inside the store
is everywhere at once
no matter where —
eternal reruns
of stray wisps of steam
that rise
from the brightly frozen,
of the canned goods and foodstuffs
stacked in columns onto columns
under columns pushed together
into walls of shelves
of aisles all celestially effacing
any trace
of bodies that have picked
packed unpacked and placed
them just so
so as to draw bodies to the
pyramid of plums,
the ziggurats
of apples and peaches and
in the bins the nearly infinite
gradations and degrees of greens
misted and sparkling.

A paradise of absence,
the dreamed-of freed
from the dreamer, bodiless
quenchings and consummations
that tomorrow will draw the dreamer
the way it draws the night tonight
to press the giant black moth
of itself against the windows
of fluorescent blazing.

Park Bench

Behind the bench the drive,
before the bench the river.
Behind the bench, white lights
approaching east and west
become red lights
receding west and east
while before the bench,
there are paved and unpaved
pathways and a grassy field,
the boathouse, and the playground, and the gardens
of a park named for a man whom
no one now remembers
except in the forgetting that occurs
whenever the park's name is said.
Left of the bench there is a bridge
that spans the river
and beyond the bridge around a bend
floodlights from the giant dry goods
that replaced the bowling alley
that replaced the slaughterhouse
are dumping fire all night long
into the river; but here
where the bench is,
the river is black, the river
is lava long past its cooling,
black as night
with only a few lights

from the upper story of the trapezoidal
five-star hotel across the water
glittering on the water
like tiny crystals in a black geode.
Haunt of courtship,
haunt of illicit tryst; of laughter
or muffled scream, what
even now years later
may be guttering elsewhere on the neural
fringes of a dream, all this
the bench is empty of,
between the mineral river that it faces
and the lights behind it speeding white
to red to white to red to white.

Downtown Strip Club

Its night is all day long;
the neon GIRLS out front go dark in sunlight,
while inside the cruciform stage
has stripped down to blackness,
in which the vertical
poles at the end of each transverse arm
stand naked and lonely.
Cold here is the cold on the faces of the presidents
on bills the absent hands
have pushed toward each body bending over
in a gown of brightness;
cold is the heat of the shadowless
shadow play of hands and legs
up and down along the poles,
and the hands retreating from the money,
and the hands in pockets dreaming,
or dreaming later on another body;
the heart of the cold is the opposite of what it is,
cold as the fire
through the day of its night
in the firing line of bottles
waiting for orders
on the shelf above the bar.

Hotel Lobby

Light the pursuer, dark the pursued.
Light wants to fill dark with itself
and have it still be dark
so light can still be filling it.
Light pours from the massive shining of the chandelier
over the bronze boy bending beneath it
to the bronze pool where a watery face
is rising to meet his as he bends.
Light the pursuer, dark the pursued,
along the naked back and arms,
the hands, the fingers reaching
for the rippling features, just
beyond, just out of the grasp of
into and out of, and across
the marble floor and pillars,
to the tips of leaves, and up
the lion claws of chair legs and sofas and
over the glass tops of tables in the lounge,
light losing dark by catching it,
dark giving light the slip by being caught,
on elevator doors, down every
blazing hallway to the highest floor,
the farthest room, and through it
beyond the pulsing colors of the muted screen,
from hip to hip in a loose twilight
of sheets no longer shifting.

Race Track

Oval of all
desire, desire's
inside track, its
fast track, ceaseless
since there is no
starting gate
no finish line,
the tote board blank,
the winner's circle empty

Phantom out of Vagrant by Unbridled

blacknesses of outdoor
betting windows
like a row of eyes
shut tight and
dreaming of the
urgent little bills
no hands shove
under the glass
across the counter —

and of the hands
too that open
all day to close
all day to open
to what's never

quite so keenly
held than in
the just before
just after

Pleasure Ride out of Nightmare by Recall

a band was playing,
the grandstand all
ablaze with flowered
dresses underneath
a preen of hats
parading in a Breeders'
Cup of bodies — was it,
could it have been
today? Just hours ago?

Whirlaway out of Day Star by Forego

Dry Cleaner

Inside the giant room
the air is like the air inside
the smallest closet,
stuffed full and locked.
The plastic wears the clothes
that wear no bodies
that hang from the inverted roller
coaster of the conveyor
that conveys them nowhere now
throughout the store
but where they are
above the yellow bins of bags
of other clothes awaiting
transport
to the big machines, the solvent
stringencies that purify them for the final
clarifying steam.
What clings
like memory to the crumpled-together sack —
cloth of pant leg
cuff or collar
tomorrow will be churned away
and pressed
into forgetfulness
till one by one the spilled-on dripped-on merely worn
will rise
in an aphasia of transparency

to sheer raiment, untouched
children again of light!
Even the numbers
tagged to belt loop lapel or label
will be a vestige only
of a vision of
that heavenly
first room before
the rooms they moved through
on their way to here,
immaculate bright showroom
in which the very eyes that looked
the hands that reached
were singing, "World
invisible, we view thee
World intangible
we touch thee
World unknowable
we know thee
Inapprehensible
we clutch thee."

Shoe Store

The new shoes not wanting to be old shoes
climb the walls;
diagonally
in diagonal rows,
there on the stalled
stair master
of each narrow shelf
shoe after shoe
is climbing undiscourageably up
to the boxes they get no closer to
stacked high above them.
They climb they plod
they run in place
all through the night
from whatever's coming
from beyond the window
across the marble
of the mall to fill them each
with alien purposes
that pass all day
below them in the carpeted scuff
and shuffle, in the wingtips
thumbed and creased
down aisles
dead-ending in a mirror.
They want to escape, these
leather infants of Sarguntum,

they want to climb back
into their boxes
under the precious tissue where,
tongue-tied
in the unlaced laces
laced together,
they can rest
in perfect darkness
forever on a shelf
too high to reach.

Stone Church

A space to rise in,
made from what falls,
from the very mass
it's cleared from,
cut, carved, chiseled,
fluted or curved
into a space
there is no end to
at night when
the stained glass
behind the altar
could be stone too,
obsidian, or basalt,
for all the light there is.

At night, high
over the tiny
galaxy of candles
guttering down
in dark chapels
all along the nave,
there's greater
gravity inside the
the grace that's risen
highest into rib
vaults and flying
buttresses, where

each stone is another
stone's resistance to
the heaven far
beneath it, that
with all its might
it yearns for, down
in the very soul
of earth where it's said
that stone is forever
falling into light
that burns as it rises,
cooling, into stone.

Playground

The fence can't even keep itself out now,
for years kicked in and bent up till
the bottom of it's curling
like a chain-link wave about to break
across the strip of grass
so it can wash away
or join the minor turbulence
of stubbed smokes, and condom
wrappers, and a beer can crushed
beside a queen of hearts
(thrown down in triumph
or defeat?).
                Beyond the grass
and moon glow of sand
under swings and the bony
gleaming of a jungle gym
grown colder every second
by forgetting all the busy
little heat of hands,
                  the blacktop is a
black hole that has
swallowed up the chalked
hearts and initials, the foursquare
boundaries and foul lines
while beyond the fence
the fence is facing
out in the street

under the streetlight
the inside of a ripped-open
half of a tennis ball
(hit or hurled?)
is blacker than the blacktop
it is tipped toward
somewhere in which
the other half is surely lying,
tipped toward the street.
Tipped, you could say, like an ear.
You could say the silence
is the sound of one ear
listening for the other
from the bottom of an
interstellar hole.
You could say sand dunes.
Aphasic metal. The breaking
chain links of a wave. At night,
in the playground,
you could say anything.

Gym

The walls are mirrors, the mirrors watch the walls
that watch the mirrors that watch the small
to large to larger barbells
that are not barbells now though ranged
in multiples of five
beside the chrome frame
of the legless leg curl and leg press,
the stacked bricks unattached
to cables, and the dry sheen
of the benches beneath the bars
beneath the lights. The room subsides,
relaxes from the room in its reflection.
Only the stairs
of the ellipticals are floating
in mid-stride but everything else
is a downward exhalation
of every breath held,
trembling, while
the iron, against its will,
was lifted, pumped, curled, or pressed,
then tremblingly set down.
The room is a downward
and inward
exhalation, the very iron breathing
into itself and through itself
to exhalations under it,

and under that,
yielding the way everything with breath yields
finally when it's breathing out.

Indoor Municipal Pool

The circulating disinfectants
make it an unearthly blue
or earth's blue seen from space,
or what pooled from the steaming
of the planet's first condensing.
In which case the pumps
and filters could be thermal
vents, and the tiny comet trail
of bubbles rising from the vents
could hold within it — if it isn't it
already — the first blind chance,
if not the promise of
the hint of the beginning
of what at long last would
emerge into the eye which
being mostly water sees
only water signaling to itself
beyond itself in accidental
wormy quiverings over
the sea floor of the ceiling.

Hospital Examination Room

The intercom is sleeping,
flashing only the red light of a dream
of no one entering
to check on no one waiting
while in the darker room
inside the mirror opposite
a red light of another dream
is flashing back.
All night, off and on,
cool air is hurried
through the floor and ceiling vents
to keep the temperature from spiking,
and while it does
until it doesn't
fresh paper, innocent of flesh,
on the examination table
rustles a little
under a phantom restlessness.
And Time too shivers
its thumbed-through
and worn-down
long-irrelevant
pages in the rack
against the wall.
And between Time and the table
from a stand,
an empty sleeve hangs

with a black tube
dangling from it
to a screen that's blank,
inside of which at the very
bottom of the blankness
sleep the numbers
of a pressure
too low to measure.

Senior Center

Light here is old, suspended
cloudy, from the cathedral ceiling,
far above the somehow brighter sheen
of its reflection on the checkered
linoleum, on the backing
and thick legs of the metal chairs
around the bridge tables,
the mahjong tables, the bingo tables —
light stumbles, it seems, it gropes,
not so much from the weight of night
against it through the sunroof
and the giant windows
as from the far-off
shining of itself
outside itself
in chairs and tables
and all across the white
checks and the black checks,
as if the source of light,
the secret, were not in light at all
but in these brighter traces
which it reaches for
the way the blind do,
baffled, feeling
the smooth braille
of every surface

for the light-encrypted
sense of what's
unreadable and clear.

Funeral Home

After the last mourners,
and the dumping out
of flowers and the polishing
and vacuuming and
sweeping up before
it starts all over again tomorrow,
a white owl keeps watch
from within his tree
within the carpet
while dust motes — stirred up
like silt in water
by the constant going
in and out all day,
the sitting and the rising —
finally reach their peak
and turn to float
back down so slowly
that the empty vases
in the dark could be
the flowers themselves,
the blossoms that have
just now opened wide
for the dry rain
that will fill them
all around the owl
on the spotless breakfront
and between the chairs

and couches and on either
side of the doorways to the
family room, the chapel,
and the roped-off staircase
which if not for the rope
could be a staircase in an inn
made to look like a home
made to look like a mansion
where no one lives.

II

GALAXY FORMATION

Triumph

I saw him as I drove by —
I don't have to tell you what he looked like —
spreading out a plastic sheet
as for a picnic
except he wasn't picnicking;
he was lying down to sleep
in the middle of the sidewalk
in the middle of the day
on a busy street,
the spoils of him lying there
for everyone to gawk at
or step around.
And when I drove by later
the same day, and then again still later
late that night,
he was still there, sleeping,
and maybe I slowed down
to check on him or got him at least a blanket,
or called an ambulance,
but whatever I did or didn't do
I did it to forget that
either way
he was the one asleep on the sidewalk,
I was the one borne along in the car
that might as well have been a chariot
of empathy, a chariot
the crowd cheers

even as it weeps

for the captured elephant too wide

to squeeze through

the triumphal arch

and draw home

to bed my sweet

sensitive Caesar of a soul.

Forgiveness

If not for her, then no one,
in the high-collared dress
with the bone-white buttons,
white as the serviette beside her,
as the teacup before her
on the dark mirror of the mahogany table
in which a shriveled
phantom of herself she isn't looking at
is floating, the hand and teacup
on the surface sinking
as she lifts the teacup to her mouth.

Hand trembling as she lifts it,
though not at all from agitation
but from a merely
neurological event
that isn't punishment
beyond the punishment in store for anyone
lucky enough to live so long.

If not for her, then no one,
steam from the teacup
delicately rising
while she speaks
not matter-of-factly
but unfazed, even defiant
looking directly at us from the screen

telling what happened sixty years ago
as if it happened to another
woman, a girl really,
just a girl she might have read about
in one of the books
that line the shelves
behind her, in a leather-bound classic
written if not for her, then whom?

The commandant's new bride
in a faraway village
that might have been
a village in a book of fairy tales,
if not for the Jews, and the stench
it was almost visible
vaporous in the last days
from across the Ettersburg
beyond the trees — you couldn't
leave the house it was so
terrible like breathing them,
their breath, and every morning
every evening
sitting down to eat
and have to see them drifting past the window,
the striped rags borne by the stench itself —
how could you

eat, how could you not
feel sorry for them,
how could you not
hate them
for how sorry they made you feel,
for the day they ruined.
I was a new bride. This was my life . . .

And only now as the tears start does she smile,
hand trembling downward as it's lifted up,
trembling upward as it sinks,
the teacup steaming delicate phantoms
all around the still defiant smile
that's also kind now, somehow,
as if she'd read our minds
and after all these years could finally
forgive everyone, see it was just
our ignorance about the many ways
there are to suffer.
She dabs her eyes, her cheeks,
and then leaning forward, looks down a moment
into the phantom face
she puts her two hands on and pushes up against,
pushing it down
away from her
to get up from the table.

Conductor

There were white mitts on his hands
to keep his hands
from pulling out the feeding tube
the IV port the catheter
and long after
he stopped communicating
he began to wave them back and forth and
up and down
as if an orchestra
that wasn't there
were playing music no one could hear
and whether because there was no score
or the absent instruments
weren't tuned or the nonexistent players
were too distracted or didn't care
the balky white mitts had to pause a lot
tapping the air people
pay attention people
before they swerved again and
dipped and paused and tapped again
all afternoon and into evening
until they got it right,
the piece entitled *Gone,*
and the white mitts could lie there
and just listen.

Edenic Simile

The way there wasn't
anything to cover up
or hide from till
they heard in the sudden
leaf shiver
and fret of gravel
the Lord approaching
through the garden
calling their name —
so, in the men's room
at the Spring Garden
Bar and Grill,
the man at the urinal —
whom I could hear
from outside singing
hunkahunka
burning love
head back (I imagined)
eyes closed waving
in perfect rhythm
to his singing
a tenor sax
of piss — stopped singing
stopped pissing
soon as he heard me
and zipped up
and looked away

as he shouldered
past me so I
in silence head bowed
could take his place
and he in silence
head bowed
before the mirror
could wash his hands,
the hands he might not
have felt the need
to wash at all
if I hadn't entered;
and when he left
there was a momentary
roaring of men and women
till the door shut,
then only the hiss
I made and the silence
of someone else
behind me waiting.

Close to You

the automatic tunes of
the codes by which
to which in which
that grease the traffic
of our gliding
all day long
unnoticeably
in and out
of view
      unlike
until a woman
spills on the counter
at the Quik Stop all
the insides of her
pocketbook and now
is scavenging
through receipts
pens tissues
and prescriptions
for the bills and loose
change she needs
to buy the smokes
she wants
            she's sorry just
a second it's here
somewhere if
we could just

give her a second
hands trembling
with the weight of
the sudden pressure from
the eyes that
because she's caught
a little short
unhoused and visible
are swarming
as to some arena
to gorge in pity
and annoyance
woe and wonder
on the spectacle
she is because
the line behind her's
getting longer
and the cashier's
fingers tap
an ever edgier
drumroll on the counter,
and above her head
up near the ceiling
Karen Carpenter
her lushly starved-
to-death angelic
voice is singing

from so far away
it's like it's trying
to keep from being
pushed out from inside
the speaker through
the tiny perforations
naked and quivering
to be let back in.

Galaxy Formation

For Reg Gibbons

In an article I'm reading in my neighborhood bar, I learn that dark
    matter, "though unseen, makes up more than 90 percent of
    the mass of the universe."

Older than visible matter, wherever dark matter has coalesced,

its gravitational force pulls stars and gases into galaxies and clus-
    ters of galaxies, and even super-clusters, holding in place what
    otherwise would wash away in the expanding universe.

I hear a woman to my right talking on her cell phone; not wanting
    to be noticed, her voice is soft but tense with what it's trying
    not to sound like, saying "Honey, listen to me, honey.
    Honey. Honey. I am not your mother. I Am Not Your Mother."
    Then she holds the phone away from her ear so even I can
    hear the tiny insect-buzzing of what against her ear would be
    his shouting back.

Starlight has to bend, the writer says, around that invisible dense
    matter,

warping itself in order to be seen.

So even after we factor in the distorting effect of time and distance,
    the light-years of light-years that light has to cross to reach

us, the visible shapes we see inside our giant telescopes look
nothing like the shapes they are.

There's a white shark on the wall next to the television screen
    where I see an aerial view of a funeral procession or a
    rally—fists shake in unison, and if the sound weren't muted
    I might hear voices chanting, but all I hear around me is a
    thick gauze of bar talk and laughter and the woman saying
    over and over, honey, honey, listen, honey, honey, while
    on the screen I continue looking up at what I'd be looking
    down on if I were there:

the massive seething a quivering cell seen under a microscope,

a dense coating of flies on something dead.

Then there's a lake, and a bright red Jeep flies out of it and lands
    safely on a dirt road and drives off right to left as if into the
    open mouth of the bright white shark.

The writer of the article describes dark matter as a black canvas
    on which the visible universe is painted. If that figure captures
    best the relationship of gloom to glitter, couldn't the canvas
    also be the painter, the unseen the conjuror of the seen, as if
    the ten percent that doesn't hide were being imagined by the
    ninety percent that does?

Dark matter. She is not his mother. She refuses to be his mother.

But there are places in the cosmos, however few and far between,
    where "galaxies form where no dark matter is, at least none we
    can detect."

In the physical therapy room of the nursing home my mother
    placed my grandmother in after she slipped in a puddle of
    urine and fell and broke her hip, the old, the damaged,
    at various stages of infirmity, were working with therapists
    at different stations in the room — one woman looked quiz-
    zically at her hand, as if it wasn't hers and wasn't not, matter
    neither dark nor bright, as it tried to squeeze a yellow ball,
    over and over, only the tips of her fingers twitching, while the
    young therapist, more girl than woman, kept urging her on the
    way a mother would,

though she was not her mother,

saying, "That's it, Lois, come on now, kiddo, you can do it, you
    did it yesterday." And nearby, a man wizened to his very bones
    held fiercely to the rails of a small track down which he took
    unsteady small step after small step, like a toddler crossing wet
    stones — he was followed by another woman with her hands
    out ready to catch him if he fell. Everywhere inside the room
    the young the healthy, the fortunate, were encouraging the

old, the sick, the hobbled — everywhere the old, eyes burn-
ing, were pushing back with all the might inside their bodies
against the dark matter their bodies had become.

Places, the writer tells me, where light too is a force, light too a
    kind of pressure

though my grandmother refused it, sitting in her wheelchair, look-
    ing on, her silence the darkest matter, an impossible density
    nothing could get around without distortion, broken only by
    her saying when my mother came to visit

You are not my daughter, I don't have a daughter,

saying it over and over, as if she knew my mother would carry
    the voice inside her ever after, beyond the funeral, no matter
    whom she spoke to, or where she went, the voice reverb-
    erating in her voice reverberating in the ones she loved, the
    ones who loved her

the distorting effects of time and distance nothing the shape it is

the white shark is swallowing the president who shakes the hand
    of another president in a bright room made brighter by the
    flash of cameras

and an old man yelling as he carries a child to some kind of safety
from a smoking doorway

the woman flips shut her phone and stuffs it in her bag and disap-
pears

and again the lake spits out the Jeep that lands safely on the
ground and drives away.

III

NIGHT OF THE REPUBLIC

Amphitheater

In the dream time
of the molecular
what persists as
colonnade
or stair is struggling
blindly to hold
back, hold
in, what in it,
of it, every
moment wants
to whirl away
from what it is.

It is a kind of keeping
faith, a loyalty,
the way the garbled
pieces of the
architrave call back
the column that's
no longer there;
how even now
the horizontal rows
of nearly worn-
away-to-nothing
seats rise steeply
all around the inside
of the colossal oval

that encloses
the missing stage
where Pindar isn't
singing, "Take heart,
remember Oedipus:
if a sharp ax
hacks off the boughs
of a great tree
so its beauty spoils and
its fruit fails,
it can still give
an account of itself
should it come later
to a winter fire,
or should it rest
at last on a foreign
pillar performing
its sad task
so far away
from what it started as."

Museum

So much of once
and now and soon
is or will soon be
caught here, framed and glassed —
free of the drifting air —
and hung, so that
the very halls
that lead from room
to room are rooms
themselves that make room
in little dim-lit alcoves
all along them for what
there wasn't room for
in the other rooms.
On the wall outside
each doorless doorway
the audio guides lined up
like black-suited
miniature docents
are waiting to tell the story
of the ambition and the breakthrough
to the early to the later
to the late or belated
recognition of the name
whose final triumph was to
end up in the digital
recording of the nameless storyteller

telling the story
to the inglorious and mute.
All night, inside each
doorway there's an empty chair
that keeps watch
over an empty bench
that watches the cordoned-
off and glassed-in
figures revert to pigments
that revert to dyes,
oils and the mineral
grains that press
against the glass
to pass right through it
into the air they came from,
alive again — docents of dispersal
drifting from room
to room through hallways
down the marble stairs
out past the headless Winged Victory
they entered by.

Bookstore

As if hallucinations made of words
could hallucinate themselves beyond the words,
out of the books, out of the newest
on display behind the window, and the ones
on tables in the gloom or ranged on shelves
in different sections; out
of the pages building to betrayal,
out of the spectral signatures
of doom of boredom of deceit,
after the stranger comes to town,
before the girl's disgrace, before
the shadowy flood or fire,
the bodiless mimicries escape
tonight the tangling plot lines
into the bodies of the couple
kissing outside the store,
into the ardor of the way they kiss,
he leaning against her leaning back
against the window, his hands flat
on the glass above her head,
hers on his hips to draw him
farther forward while her leg rubs
up the inside of his thigh
and down, and up again,
higher and still higher,
while the books behind them keep their own sweet time,
serene because the wraiths return,

inevitably, tomorrow or next week
or years away and a cooler hand
will take the book and open to a passion much
more desolate for being mutual
and new and never ending
till the page is turned.

Barbershop

"Beauty falls from the air."
— *Thomas Nashe*

Eternity is the spiral up the pole
spiraling to its endless end.
Time is the vitrine
of antiquated gels,
conditioners, restoratives,
stray sections from yesterday's *Today*
all over the table
in the waiting area where
Eternity is waiting.
Time is the electric
razors upright in their chargers
beside their teeth-like
attachments, and the scissors,
the clippers, the trimmers,
on the mirrored shelves
attached to mirrors
that the big chairs face,
unswiveling.
              Eternity
is the swept floor,
the bald air,
the faceless mirrors,
while Time, and its one idea
of beauty falling,

is a book of blank pages
ghostwritten by
Eternity in vanished
passages of hair.

Post Office

A convex mirror tilts downward from the corner
where wall and ceiling meet
behind the nearly room-length counter.
In the center of the mirror
what's beyond the counter
bends a smaller version of itself above the counter
out toward itself below it
while the room's periphery
curves back into the dark
the center's bending from.
Parallel to the counter
the rope barrier
strung straight from post to post
curls into itself within the mirror,
though parallel to it and just as long
but too far back beyond the mirror's border
to be caught within it
there is a narrow table
with pens at intervals
that hang at the ends
of silver chains
or lie in a silver tangle on the surface —
while one chain dangles penlessly
like a silver snake's sloughed skin.
The mirror is a little world, a globe, a map.
Back against the far wall
there's a wider table

for the giant book
of everywhere
and slots and holders for every size
and kind of envelope or label
all of which tonight are unaware
of the out-of-the-blue
or dreaded plea plaint news
or notices they'll be tomorrow —
And if the mirror is a map
this table is the blank space
on which the mapmaker scrawls — Here Be Monsters.
Here be indecipherable codes,
unreachable addresses,
every letter a dead letter,
unclaimed, untracked,
from no from
to no to.

Convention Hall

There was the amplified and echoing
"optimistic hatred of the actual"
that every flag waving
to make it so kept
waving to the joyous rhythm of
even after
in the docile chaos of a
confetti of balloons
tumbling out of darkness
high above the lights.

Look at Us, the anthem,
Look at Us, the shield,
the sacrifice —
    but look
at how unfillable
the cavern of the Great Hall is,
more vacant and silent
for the stage dismantled,
the massive absence
of the cheering and singing; look
at how the last of us,
our delegate
    torch in hand
sleepwalks in patrol
patrolling nothing
like a soldier "in the

midst of doubt, in
the collapse of creeds"
who doesn't know
the war has ended,
behind enemy lines
no longer there,
obedient to "a cause
he little understands,
in a campaign
of which he has
no notion, under
tactics of which
he doesn't see the use" —
moving in darkness
from light to smaller light
along the catwalks
through the tunnels
over the swept floor
to the farthest exit sign.

Government Center

All of the old buildings that surround it
with their embellishments,
their frills, their flauntings,
have turned away, embarrassed
by how nakedly
outside

        outside is here.
At night especially,
nothing is not exposed
to whatever it is
that's looking out
from within the rising of the set-back
or jutting, many-angled
brick and concrete large
to small to smaller openings
that swallow
whatever light they cast.
At Washington and State,
the wide brick stairs lead up to wide brick stairs
up to the bricked
expanse, the brick field of the benchless plaza
edged here and there by lampposts whose light
spotlights the little public trees
that tremble leafless
and raw in stone tubs
for everyone

who isn't there
to see.

If you were there, walking,
you wouldn't be able to tell
the sound of other footsteps
coming toward you
were your own.
You'd have to hurry not to feel
the feeling of what it is
you're being told
about the feeling of being
looked at, looked through, tracked
by every brick
and concrete
angle of the opaque
openings you can't look up at
                              into
as you hurry past.

Courtroom

Hillsborough, North Carolina

Everything inside the room
looks upward
through penumbral zones
from the ghost ship of the gallery's
galley-rows of benches to the
waist-high balustrade
that is the barrier
we call the Bar, and from
the tables beyond the Bar
to the lectern facing
the high desk
we call the Bench,
behind which
above the flag we call the Flag,
high on the wall to where
the circle of the seal is
across the bottom of the outer
rim of which
the legend in a language
no one speaks
is speaking silently to no one:
Esse Quam Videri — To Be
Rather Than to Seem —
Like what? the two girls
staring out inside the seal
appear to ask, like what?

in white robes —
Greek or Roman, Roman or Indian?
a Roman's seal's Greek fantasy
of an Indian princess and her attendant,
the princess seated
on a tree stump, on a beach,
the water calm behind her,
as she looks down
past the Bench, the Bar, the strict rows
of low benches in the gallery
where the absent galley slaves
lashed to the public oars
are rowing nowhere
and so can't notice
that a ship over her shoulder
(is it the ship they row?)
is sailing straight for the horn of plenty
spilling the goods out
in profuse disorder at her feet.
Like what if not like here
at night where the improbable
is law, and logic
a penumbral state in which "tar heels"
from Ohio could be "first in flight"
above a beach named after a bird
named after a cat.

The Public

The no one of it
is everywhere.
It is a high-rise that
is itself a wall
of windows all
but one of which
halfway up is dark,
rising above the locked
gate against which
a stray page of the day's
disasters has been
blown flat, trembling
against the iron
bars as if trying
to pass through or
over them, like a
fugitive the dogs
are closing in on,
wanting in, wanting
for God's sake someone
to take him in, as if
that sole blue light
above were safety,
except it isn't
safety, is it,
it's the news

on television, the same
news of the same
day — it is news
calling out to news
as pixel to print
to pixel over circuits
and atonal airways
that someone earlier
left on before leaving
to make it seem
as if someone were home.

IV

AT THE CORNER OF
COOLIDGE AND CLARENCE

For Tom Sleigh

Beloved

The block is empty. I'm the boy there in the street,
Looking downhill for you to turn the corner,
Out of the avenue where horn blare, veils

Of exhaust, and strangers in a hurrying sleepwalk
Through each other tell me you'll be here soon.
And soon is home, and home is when at last

Your any moment now sensation brings
Out of the day's dull glint and inching flow
The look and bearing of a just for me

Unearned, unjustified, imagined face
That's all I need, so long as it's arriving,
That's mine till your real face effaces it.

But not today, not now, not ever again.
No one but me is left here outside the house
Where you by being dead are more alive

To me than ever, you who have no other
Purpose now, no other way of being,
Than to appear by never quite appearing,

Whenever I need you, any time I want
Clearer and still clearer in the aftermath
Of your not yet but soon about to happen.

Flowerpot

I lay back on the carpeted bottom step
Of the stairwell that like a well extended
Darkly up to the window near the ceiling,

Up where the china man under the wide-brimmed hat
That hid his face pulled the flowerpot that held
No flower across the sill no one could reach.

There was a television on somewhere
Above me, and the doomsday clock was ticking,
Someone was saying. Someone was saying something

About a blockade and a quarantine,
Who would blink first, lose face, or push the button.
A fat man banged a shoe against a desk.

The china man however didn't care.
Pulling his flowerpot of absent flowers,
He was content to be a clot of darkness

Brightening the moment late sun caught the glass —
The hat tip first, and then the hat, the arms,
The rickshaw of the flowerpot he pulled.

And everywhere within the light's slow fall
Infinities of particles were falling
Into the flowerpot they'd never fill.

The Family

Three million years ago, three barefoot people —
A father and mother and a little child —
Were walking close together in moist ash.

I saw their footprints in a photograph —
The child walked beside his mother, the father
A step or two ahead, and it was raining,

Fat raindrops pocked the ash around their feet,
The ash that later hardened under ash
Preserved in ash the way the mother paused,

Turned left a moment, not sure where she should go,
Looking behind her at the home she fled?
At the volcano exploding in the distance?

Anonymous as Lot's wife, turning around —
In sorrow or relief? As if a blank
Impenetrable cloud, extending back

In time forever opened only there
Just then, and briefly, for only ninety feet,
Before it closed again for good behind them,

Whoever they were, wherever they were going,
On a rainy day three million years ago,
Walking together barefoot in the ash.

Light Switch

The bad news was the sun was mortal too.
One day it would just burn out. The good news was
We'd all be long gone by the time it happened.

The good news was there wasn't any place
Inside the house I couldn't find extinctions
To study and by studying prepare

Myself for what I wouldn't live to see:
The way the angry little ball of fire
From a struck match would vanish when I shook it

Into a loosening skeleton of smoke;
Or how the world that watched me from the TV screen
Swallowed itself the moment I turned it off.

The good news was the light switch in my room,
The way I'd flick it on and off so quickly
That when the room went black an after-room

Lit by a spectral light would drift on the blackness,
The bed, the desk, the streetlamp in the window,
Drifting before me till the black seeped through.

I watched it till it wasn't anymore
To feel as if I understood. That was
The good news. The bad news was it did no good.

Sickbed

There were two voices in the fever dream:
Hers speaking from another room, and theirs,
The teenyboppers', singing from the screen.

Hers spoke a litany of grievous thanks,
And thankful worries, who did what to whom,
And why, and thank God it wasn't worse, poor bastard,

Poor thing, while theirs kept singing who wears short
Shorts, we wear short shorts, over and over
Till I was singing too. Someone, thank God, at last,

Was out of it, and someone else, thank God,
Had only lost a breast, and Shirley what
A good kid, what a beauty, what a doll,

She let herself go when the bum walked out.
Thank God they never had a child. Thank God
They smelled the smoke; they found the keys, the dog.

Thank God they all wore short shorts as they sang
To me on little stages on the stage
Where boys and girls were dancing all around them,

Singing and dancing where it wasn't worse,
Thank God, and, thank God, no one paused to wonder
Who to thank for just how bad it was.

Coffee Cup

Consider the cup of coffee, black as night,
At night, all night, beside her on the table,
Under the kitchen light where she would sit

Staring at nothing, still as a photograph.
Consider the way at first the steam would rise,
Like phantoms twisting up against each other

Struggling to pull away from the black lake
That burned them every which way into nothing.
Consider the cup of coffee as it cooled,

The glassy black of it on which the light
Above floated a tiny version of itself.
How like an eye it might have looked to her,

The bright pupil there, the negative of hers,
If she had seen it, although she never did,
Never so much as lifted up the cup,

Never so much as touched it, staring off
At nothing as it went from hot to cold,
To colder while you watched her from the hallway,

Back in the dark beyond the doorway's frame,
Unseen, unseeable, and completely safe
As the cold eye in the mirror of the cup.

Cigarette Smoke

The cigarette leaning in the ashtray's groove,
On the side table beside the easy chair,
Before the never-turned-off television,

Released a single strand of smoke straight up
In a slender column that looked like it would go
On stretching in a straight line to the ceiling,

Though always at the same point — maybe a foot
Or so above the ashtray — it would waver,
And bend and branch, the branches branching too,

Thinning to veins, the veins to capillaries
Entangling and knotting up each other
Into a bluish opalescent cloud.

There had to be a reason why it split
And whorled and tangled in that slow turbulence,
And why the cloud it turned into would rise

Just so high and then hang there like a halo
Under the lamplight just above her head,
While on the screen a movie star who'd died

Was somehow standing on a subway vent
And laughing as she tried to hold her white
Dress down against the wind that lifted it.

Piano Bench

Back in an alcove off the upstairs room,
Against the wall, the tall piano slept
Beside the record player that had no needle,

Beside a crate of albums. The tall piano slept,
And nobody would wake it. Under the lid
Too heavy for me to lift, the keys would dream

All day of songs in the piano bench,
Locked up on sheets of paper, behind bars,
The way the records locked up their songs as well

Inside the tight cell of concentric grooves
I'd hold a fingernail to just to see
If I could spring them while the record spun.

The piano slept, and nobody could wake it.
Nobody could stop the keys under the lid
From dreaming all the melodies they dreamed

When no one else was home, in the empty house,
When the radio and the TV downstairs
Were sleeping too, the silence through the day

Now like a round of voiceless voices all
Around me singing songs I couldn't hear
While the turntable turned under my finger.

Dryer

I sat before the porthole to watch the clothes
Billowing and collapsing round and round
For hours inside the perforated drum.

As if I watched the world from outer space,
In an accelerated sky, white clouds
Of underwear and T-shirts massed and parted,

Slid away to mass again, in never quite
The same white vortices within vortices
You couldn't see down to the bottom of.

I watched geologies of color, deep time
Of mountain ranges rising from a sea
They just as quickly sank into again;

Pangaea breaking into continents,
Continents into islands, and the islands
Into that reef of blue cuff, green peninsula

Of pant leg, flashing up and driven down,
Churning itself upon itself, in cycles
Neither different nor the same, over

And over for five billion years until
The bell rang as the drum stopped, and it all
Fell past the porthole into what it was.

Bathtub

Aside from sleep, there were two ways to practice:
One was to lie back in the bath and stay there
Still as the stillest water my stillness made

Until I couldn't feel it anymore,
The heat of it, despite how hot it was.
As if my body had become no body,

Suspended in a nothing that could turn
Back into burning only when I moved.
The other way was picturing the pink

Gum hard as marble someone I didn't know
Had left on the bottom of my desk at school,
The desk carved with initials no one knew,

Forgotten, in that row of desks inside
That classroom in a vast hall of classrooms
On the third floor of the elementary school

At three o'clock on Sunday in the thick
Of summer when the bell rings for no reason,
And the silence in the moment after

Is suddenly everywhere an avalanche
Of silence that in the moment after that
Becomes again the silence that it is.

Family Pictures

At first it was the old dead on the wall
Above the fireplace nobody lit,
Who kept watch on the empty living room;

Solemn or smiling, who never looked away
From the fluffed cushions of the reading chair,
The glass-topped coffee table where a stack

Of *Mona Lisa* coasters lay beside
A giant picture book nobody opened.
All day and night, they watched the plastic-covered

Couches that I was not to sit on ever,
The crystal goblets I was not to touch
Behind a locked door in the cabinet

Where silver hid inside a felt-lined box.
And then each year, it seemed, more dead would join them,
Some old, some younger, some my parents' age,

And even one or two my own, in clothes
I could imagine wearing, seeing myself
Up there among them keeping a close eye too

On everybody coming after me
Who needed to be reminded constantly
That nothing in the living room was theirs.

Color

How did God move? And anyway why would he?
Where would he go, where could he ever need
To go if he was everywhere already?

How could I think of it, or picture it —
God moving "over the blank face of the void" —
Except as color, instantaneous as color?

And what was color really but a vital
Absence living where it was and wasn't,
Insolid soul of visibility,

The unseen of seeing all at once and too
Continuously for the eye to see
The trackless path it traces to the eye:

The finch's yellow now-there-not-there flashing
Among the leaves, and the leaves too, their green
Degrees, gradations, shifting moods, a green

Or yellow fire unfixed and alive
And flaring out indifferent to the sight
It woos and enters, indifferent to the bird,

The leaf, the very air it all at once
Continuously dwells in and deserts,
Awake and wakeless, light-borne, born of light?

Faucet

The faucet dripped one slow drip from its lip,
A slight convexity at first of metal
Distilled from metal to a silvery blur,

Opaque as mercury, that thickened to
A see-through curvature, a mound that swelled
As streams I couldn't see poured in and filled it,

Stretched by its own weight to a rounder shape
That grew less round the heavier it grew,
A tiny sack of water filled by water,

Held by water trembling as it clung
And dangled, swaying, till it snapped in two,
And one part plummeted and the other sprung

Back to the lip and grew all over again.
I told myself if I could just remember
The way the trembling surface tension full

Of surface tension hung there till it didn't,
Till it did again, somehow the house,
And everything and everyone within it,

The very moment of that day and year,
All of it, every bit would return to me
Exactly as it was. And I did. And it didn't.

Bedroom Door

The book informed you that the universe,
Infinite though it was, was still expanding
Though into where or what it didn't say.

You didn't need it to, it didn't matter,
Feeling space all around you moving off
The longer you stood there in the hall to hear

Their voices arguing behind the door,
One moment shouting and the next imploring,
Complaining, berating, don't take that tone with me,

See what you've done, you happy now, you happy?
Words flying beyond their meaning into sound
That flew in turn beyond sound into echoes

And after echoes you could feel, not hear.
And feel more keenly the farther away they flew.
The universe expanded to make room

For all the outer space their voices were creating,
Till even what was nearest moved away,
Till there was nothing near, and everywhere

In all directions all at once was rushing
Forever from the shrinking dot of your
Attention into who knew what or where.

Solitaire

The flip, flip, flip of card on tabletop,
The flat hiss of the cards her hands were sliding
From column to column as the columns grew

And shrank, and shrank and grew, by suit and sequence,
Her face unsmiling, fixed in its staring down
At the unsmiling faces of the queen,

The king, the jack that stared back up at her
From the wrong column, or the wrong order,
The royal family broken apart and scattered,

Unable without her help to reunite.
That's why she played for hours, sometimes all night,
To prove to them how much they need her, how

There'd be no family till she got it right.
Would it kill them, for once, to thank her for this devotion,
The slid cards hissing, the flip, flip, flip,

While down the hall that wasn't a hall at all
But a rope bridge over a gorge in the antipodes
I huddled before the snowy screen where Ralph,

The Honeymooner, shook his fist and said,
One of these days, Alice, one of these days —
Bang! Zoom! To the moon! And people laughed.

Cellar

They said the boy who lived here in my room
Before I did came home one day from school
And hanged himself from a hook in the cellar wall.

They said he left no note. They said he showed no signs
Of being blue — that's what they called it then —
They said the day was just another day

In just another week on a quiet street
Where nothing ever happened, until this did
And the family sold the house and moved away.

They never said the cellar was to blame,
The metal door slanted against the house
That led by steep steps down into the black

Of it that slowly as your eyes adjusted
Became a pit of dark and darker shadows
The darkest of which was the dead furnace

In a far corner, a dank cold smell of ash
Surrounding it as if to warn you off,
And there beside the furnace a chainless bike

With fat flat tires, and above the bike
The hook below a narrow window that
The cut grass grew against and covered up.

White Gloves

Nothing as soft as the silk-lined leather gloves
Kept in the top drawer of her dresser, the black ones
And the cream ones, the slip-ons or the buttoned,

Laced-up or ruched, the flared, the elbow-length,
The heavy stifling odor of lilac and something
Talcum-like that rose from the open drawer,

Lustre of the red Dents, flat sheen of the Pittards,
Day in day out, for high and low occasions,
Until the last occasion, whatever it was,

When none of them were ever worn again,
Not even the white ones, the most expensive,
The ones she buried at the bottom of the drawer

That I would now and then dig out and look at,
As if by looking at the pattern of
The stitching or the textures of the grain,

I'd understand the meaning of the pictures
Of the president suddenly reaching for his throat,
And the first lady turning to look at him,

Turning to see what's wrong when the head explodes,
And she's crawling out across the back of the car
In a pink dress suit, pink hat and bright white gloves.

Shed

A cat jumped out of the shed when I opened it,
And from far away inside a startled room
Inside me that I didn't know was there,

Somebody screamed, and it was only then
I understood exactly what it meant,
The science book that told me I was made

Of cells, and the cells were made of molecules
Made of atoms made of mostly space,
And how within what wasn't space within them

There were other spaces, smaller and vaster spaces,
And somewhere within them all there was this room,
And somebody inside the room was screaming.

He screamed so far away across the outer
Reaches of all that inner space, light-years
Of emptiness between himself and me,

That the scream itself was like the light
Of stars that had vanished long before the light
Had ever reached my eyes. So while the boy

Screamed, and would not stop screaming, how could I tell him
That it was just a cat that had jumped out
From the shed, a cat, and now the cat was gone?

Hallway

You could stand in the hallway between rooms,
Between belonging anywhere, and feel
As if you were the wind harp of the house

That the voices played, trembling inside you,
If you were quiet enough, unseen enough,
Your nerve ends, tuned to their very tips

To every spoken and unspoken mood,
Discordant mutterings and "the random gales"
Of love cries, curses you could always feel,

If not quite hear, above the laugh track or
The gunfire or the talking talk-show host
They turned up high to hide themselves behind.

You were the wind harp of the listening house;
You were the open instrument the voices
Swept across, not knowing that they did,

The taut strings of your attention trembling
Long into what has long since disappeared
From the dark hallway that is nowhere now

But here in these lines where you feel the air
Of every lost voice quickening again
Across the mute harp they never knew was there.

The Doorbell

The doorbell rang an eight-note melody,
And if I didn't hurry down the stairs
To the front door before the eighth note played,

I told myself there'd be nobody there.
The world impatient to be unaware
Of me again would never bring them back.

Why else would that eighth note linger in the stairwell,
Drawing itself out to its last vibration
Except to wait for me, keeping time away,

Turning the present moment to a birth-
Day present my every quick step down the stairs
Brought nearer till the front door opened it?

And even now I hear it, note after note
Of the old melody whose last note pauses
In the no time of my hurrying down

To get to you, in time, whoever you were,
You who I am now, whom I have become,
The one the world's impatient to take back,

The one behind the door who's pushed the button,
And waits there listening for the sound
Of anybody's footstep coming near.

NOTES

"Dry Cleaner": the closing lines are by James Thomson.

"Close to You": from "Close to You," a hit single by the Carpenters in the 1970s.

"Amphitheater": the quotation is based on Pindar's fourth Pythian ode (lines 262–268).

"Convention Hall": the second line is quoted from Martha Nussbaum's *Love's Knowledge* (page 213); "in the midst of doubt . . ." is from Oliver Wendell Holmes's essay on the Civil War.

"Hallway": the quoted phrase is from Coleridge's "Aeolian Harp."